MIDNIGHT MILES

POCKET BOOKS

NEW YORK / LONDON / TORONTO / SYDNEY

MAROON 5
MIDNIGHT MILES

ON THE ROAD THROUGH 5 CONTINENTS & 17 COUNTRIES. *(with Quotes Overheard On the Road)*

PHOTOGRAPHS BY CHRISTOPHER WRAY-MCCANN.
INTRODUCTION BY GRAHAM NASH.

 BOOKS

POCKET BOOKS

NEW YORK / LONDON / TORONTO / SYDNEY

ACKNOWLEDGMENTS

SPECIAL THANKS TO:
Chris Wray-McCann, Peter Young, Graham Nash,
Gabe Kuo, Masha Nova, and Jacob Hoye.

CREDITS
EDITED BY JACOB HOYE.
DESIGNED BY THE BRM.
HANDWRITING BY UNIVERSALCONSCIENCE.

POCKET BOOKS

POCKET BOOKS, a division of Simon & Schuster, Inc. 1230 Avenue of the Americas, New York, NY 10020

Text copyright © 2006 by Adam Noah Levine, Jesse Royal Carmichael,
James Burgon Valentine, Ryan Michael Dusick, and Michael Allen Madden

Photographs copyright © 2006 by Christopher Wray-McCann

MTV Music Television and all related titles, logos,
and characters are trademarks of MTV Networks,
a division of Viacom International Inc.

ISBN-13: 978-1-4165-2419-9
ISBN-10:   1-4165-2419-3

This MTV Books/Pocket Books trade paperback edition July 2006

10 9 8 7 6 5 4 3 2 1

POCKET and colophon are registered trademarks of Simon & Schuster Inc.

Manufactured in China

For information regarding special discounts for bulk purchases, please contact
Simon & Schuster Special Sales at 1-800-456-6798 or business@simonandschuster.com

INTRODUCTION

THE MID-MORNING LIGHT over the grounds of the Brentwood School in Los Angeles set the scene for the graduation of my son, Jackson. The year was 1997. The month was July. Over in one corner of the field, a group of young kids was setting up their musical equipment. Seeing this sent me way back to when I had done the very same thing a thousand times with my first professional band, the Hollies. Yes, I'd been there, done that, and I knew the feeling well. Did they have all the amps, drums, guitars, bass, and piano stuff they needed? Did they have all the wires and pedals and connections necessary to be able to perform? They had played small shows before but this was the first gig I'd seen and they were not only going to play in front of their parents but also, possibly more importantly, their friends. They may have also been slightly nervous knowing that I was there. After all, my band, Crosby, Stills and Nash, were a large presence in the music scene. At this point in their lives, their band was called Kara's Flowers, and I immediately recognized two things: one, their music was very promising for a new band, and, two, they had the passion. All the rehearsing in the world will do no good if you don't have the passion to want to communicate your thoughts and feelings through your music. I knew that whatever "it" was, they had it. I decided to keep in touch with them and see how they developed.

One day I asked my son, Will, and my daughter, Nile, how the band was doing, and Will told me that the group was frustrated and disappointed in how their musical lives were going. That "big break" hadn't come along and they were thinking of giving up and getting on with the rest of their lives. This didn't sit well with me because I knew from my own experience that sometimes all it takes is one person believing in and encouraging a band to make that critical difference. I asked Will to suggest that I fund a trip back into the studio to give it one last shot. It worked. The demos they made with my producers Russell and Nathaniel Kunkel got everything headed in the right direction. They changed their name to Maroon 5 and the rest, as they say, is history.

Here before you is a visual representation of the life of a true brotherhood of music. These pictures brilliantly show the band completely immersed in their music and thoroughly enjoying performing for millions of their fans. This book of images by Christopher Wray-McCann places you right there with them on an intimate trip through the world of Maroon 5.

Enjoy this book and this journey. I know I did.

Graham Nash
January 25, 2006
Jodhpur, India

CONTENTS

USA → 8
AUSTRALIA → 74
BRAZIL → 90
JAPAN → 100
UK → 124
EUROPE → 162
N. AMERICA → 232

USA

it's all PRetty Much the Same Until we get there.

every Night could Be so Much Fun.

It's OK,
we're going Round the BACK WAY, You KNow, the "ARtists enTRance"

- What did you buy?

it's Just a DooRs album foR when I get DRUNK oR miss L.A.
which happens a Lot.

- <u>THAT</u> is a violation.

NO MAN, it's the Real Deal.

→ MICKEY

ON TOUR, I HAVE NO IDEA what it's like to be home, and conversely, having been home for months now, I have barely any sensory recollection of being on tour. The last three years are a blur of peanut butter and jelly sandwiches, hotel porn, meet-and-greets, airport lounges, vans, a very unaccommodating RV, bus drivers, and streams of whiskey. And, of course, countless shows that now feel like individual pieces of one giant, Sisyphean concert. Certain distinguishing events fight to the surface of my memory, like hiking in Muir Woods or visiting the site of the Cabaret Voltaire in Zurich, but even these are gauzy and distant. The photographs in this book tell a much better story than I can, and, rather than serve as Proustian triggers, they have become a series of frozen moments unto themselves, to the point that I barely feel that I'm looking at myself when I see them (particularly if it's a picture of, say, James. Ha.). So, herein is a version of life on the road with Maroon 5. I'm told it's very accurate.

(we circle in the night and are consumed by the fire)

- where are you from?

i'm from the 70's.

- Do we have to watch
the jazz documentary?

No, you can go to the
BACk of the BUs.

It's an interesting feeling really, to scroll through all the numbers in your cellphone and realize there is no one who will ~~understand~~ understand.

AGENDA

OCT 3 03

★ WELCOME ★

★ BONE HEADS ★

I Don't want to Live in a Utopian Society. How BoRing.

girls Assume the worst
and expect the Best.

Sometimes I just don't want to talk to anyone.

MAYBe we can go to a BathRoom with a RestauRant attached?

IF YOU KNOW where YOU'Re going and You KNOW where You are, then You can't Be LosT.

SOME of MY BeST FRiends ARe PARt of the Jewish Media coNspiRacy.

AUST RALIA

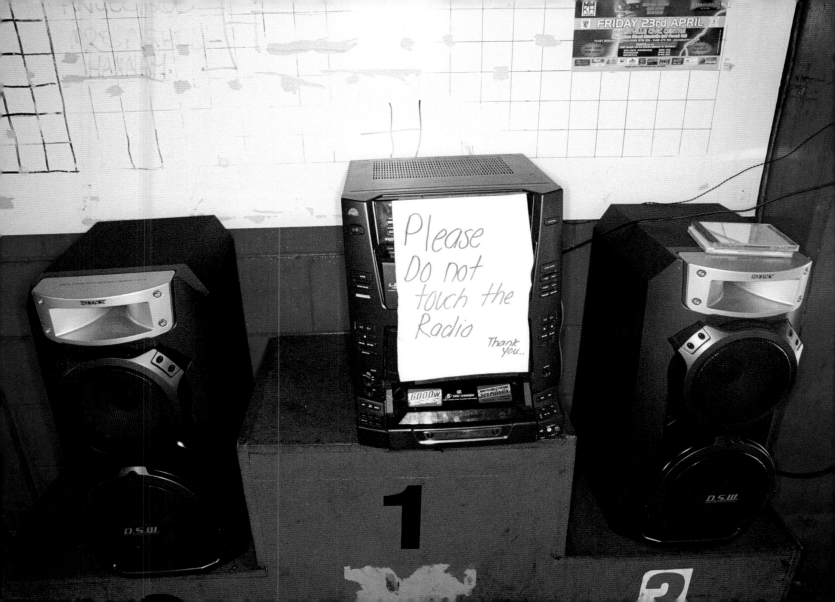

Whenever I can tell you that Jesus is my Savior, I will.

RYAN

"... it was the season of Light, it was the season of Darkness, it was the spring of hope, it was the winter of despair ..." ~ *Charles Dickens*

THE LIFE OF A TOURING MUSICIAN ISN'T FOR EVERYONE. At some point I had to condition myself to believe that living on the road was a natural existence. I think I can speak for most of the band in saying that we all had to shift our sensibilities a bit to get used to the circus lifestyle, and in one way or another we all lost our minds in the three-and-a-half-year touring cycle for *Songs About Jane.*

Our good friend Chris Wray-McCann recently used an analogy to describe my life over the last few years that I found appropriate enough to borrow. Everyone's life swings between extremes like a pendulum, and life essentially consists of a series of hills and valleys that comprise the essence of our experience. He added that my circumstances in particular caused my pendulum to swing ten times farther in each direction than the

84

average person. Due to these extremes, I feel as though I've experienced a lifetime of joy and pain in the span of a few short years. Between the time that we started making the album in 2001 and the time the album reached the crest of its success in 2004, we went from being starving musicians wondering what the future held to riding a wave of success beyond our wildest expectations. We experienced fulfillment on a level few people ever reach with opportunities to do things about which most people only fantasize. My enjoyment of these incredible experiences, however, was tempered by agonizingly painful experiences along the way.

As we hit the road in 2002, I geared myself up for what I anticipated would be a long haul. I was determined to enjoy the experience regardless of its outcome. I was excited to see the world, to live as a band of gypsies, floating from town to town in a van with only our instruments in tow. Having lived in an apartment with five other people in college, I was prepared for the conditions of living in tight quarters. We took turns driving and sleeping, playing in every city where a band of our type could perform, often to nonexistent crowds. We went to local radio stations and played acoustically, trying to foster some kind of interest in the band, often brushing our teeth in the parking lot before entering the studio. Sleep was a precious commodity, often done on the floor of the van. Food of any quality was hard to come by, as was a clean place to bathe. That said, it was still one of the best years of my life. We paid our dues and by the start of 2003, we were headlining gigs in small clubs around the country. It was a real grassroots campaign, and I felt fulfilled knowing that our growing success was the product of hard work and determination.

As we coasted through 2003, the sky truly seemed to be the limit. We lined up a couple of large summer tours opening for very successful artists, and we were slowly building a loyal fan base. We played our first arena show, opening for John Mayer, an exhilarating experience to say the least. Toward the end of the set, Adam asked the lighting guy to bring up the house lights, and there we were, standing in front of ten thousand people, all of whom were paying attention to our music. It felt so much like a dream that I actually started laughing out loud. After a few promotional trips to London, we did our first overseas tour of Europe in the fall of 2003. As amazing as it was to see some of the most beautiful places in the world, I had experienced true exhaustion for the first time. Jetlag wreaks havoc on my constitution and performing without sleep is difficult. I took it in stride, however, as this was a once-in-several-lifetimes opportunity to do what I had always dreamed of doing—playing music for a living, traveling the globe, and doing it all with a good group of friends that had stuck together since we were teenagers.

When we returned from Europe to start our first full-length headlining tour of the States, everything came to a head. I was utterly exhausted and jet-lagged to an unreasonable degree, yet our first single was finally starting to take off, and our first show was in Los Angeles. It was a homecoming. There was no time to rest. In fact, our schedule only intensified. We played three sold-out nights at the House of Blues, with TV appearances early each day, and by the end of the third show my right arm was shaking so hard I was incapable of signing my own autograph. By the middle of the tour, exhaustion, intense pain in my right arm, and subsequently deteriorating coordination playing the drums rendered me unable to continue. There we were, finally beginning to experience the success for which we had worked and dreamed about so long, and I couldn't keep up. Before I took my first break from touring, I lived with the daily anguish of knowing that it was just a matter of time before my body would give out on me. Every show was a rush of adrenaline and pain, excitement and agony.

I finally went home for a week to rest, flying in our good friend, Ryland Steen, to take my place for a few shows. When I returned I was so determined to rise above the pain that I somehow managed to keep it together through the end of the tour. Actually, some of those final shows stand among my favorites, particularly one night at the legendary Fillmore Theater in San Francisco. Despite Jesse's 104° fever, we were at the top of our game. After two years of touring, the energy of our live performance was just hitting its highest stride. I judge a concert by the amount of songs in the set that capture the true spirit of the compositions. That night, every song felt right to me. In a place as beautiful as the Fillmore, I felt humbled to be playing music so well. We had completed our first successful tour and were elated.

We carried that feeling into 2004 and I enjoyed some of the most incredible moments of my life early that year, the first of which was a performance at Clive Davis's pre-Grammy celebration. Clive's party is a huge occasion every year with a guest list the likes of which is unparalleled. It was our coming-out party so to speak, and it was nerve-racking but exhilarating. We walked onstage to a front row consisting of Jay-Z, Missy Elliot, P. Diddy, Jermaine Dupri, Terry Lewis and Jimmy Jam, and an audience that included Carlos Santana, Robbie Robertson, Dave Matthews, and Slash, among other luminaries. We played two songs and received praise from some of our biggest heroes. What could be more fulfilling than receiving recognition from some of the very people who inspire you? Next up was *Saturday Night Live*. Our performance on that show was the moment at which we realized we had made it. We were glowing, recalling all the artists that had performed on that stage over the years. We knew that no matter what, nobody could ever take that away from us. It was validation on a level we couldn't have anticipated.

Sadly, my difficulties performing lingered. We had another long year of touring ahead of us, and I did anything I could to avoid pondering the worst. We kicked off another European tour with promises of a break when we got home, but it was not to be. When we received our "revised" itinerary, we were at the airport in Milan, and I broke down. I saw another break evaporate and I could barely function. I knew I was near the end and it wouldn't be long before my grip would fail. From there we went to Australia, where my exhaustion and pain reached new depths, and then straight into a college tour of the States, during which my performances were feeble at best.

Halfway through that tour, I deteriorated to such a degree that both of my arms were pretty much useless. Josh Day, who was drumming for opening act Sara Bareilles, was kind enough to sit in for me while I went home to undergo tests and physical therapy, expecting to have to miss a couple months of touring. There we were, enjoying ever more success, achieving unbelievable things, and I was on my way home. Over the next nine months I underwent every kind of exam and therapy imaginable, all the time thinking about the band performing without me. Matt Flynn, whom we had met when he was playing with Gavin DeGraw, assumed the drumming duties. No one could get a firm grip on what had gone wrong and how it could be resolved. Diagnoses from different doctors came and went, from Chronic Tendonitis to Thoracic Outlet Syndrome (which basically means the arms don't work right) to Chronic Nerve Impingement. All I knew is that I couldn't play the drums.

It was awful, but I tried to remain optimistic. At the start of 2005 we were nominated for a Grammy and were invited to open the broadcast. This was the pinnacle. I set my sights on this performance as my triumphant return. I willed as much physical fitness as I could and practiced as much as my body would allow. When it came time to rehearse for the show, however, it was clear that I would not be able to hack it. Playing through pain as long as I had, I developed improper mechanics—a huge setback. I would essentially need to relearn how to play the drums.

As the band with which I had worked so hard and so long played on one of the biggest stages in the world, I sang my back-up vocals from the monitor board as I had a few times before, while another man played my parts. It was the zenith of success and validation, and my biggest heartbreak.

Another year of touring passed, of which I participated in about half, though I never played the drums onstage again. The pendulum swings back and forth every day, between the incredible success of the album and my agonizing inability to perform. Over this period of my life I have experienced highs and lows the likes of which people write books about. As the touring cycle finally closes, I count my blessings and look to the future as a time to learn from my past.

BRAZIL

No Dude, the wild goose is Right here.

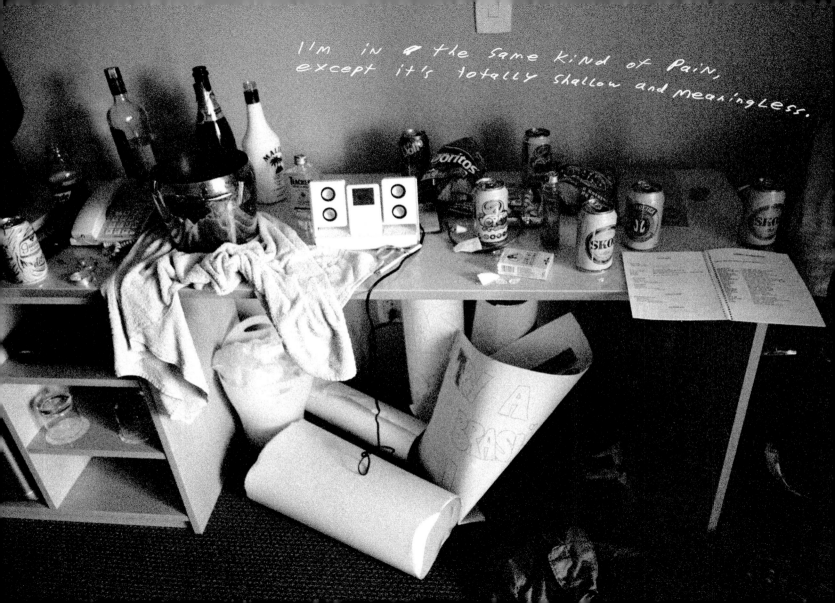

JAPAN

注 意 事 項

一、楽屋の管理は使用者側で行って下
　さい。楽屋での物品の紛失には責
　任を負いかねますので、貴重品
　の取扱いには特に注意して下さ
　い。

二、楽屋内の備品は他へ持ち出
　で下さい。

三、電熱器

四、さ
　す

五、そ
　事務所

I want to Fuck up my own Jeans, is that too much to ask?

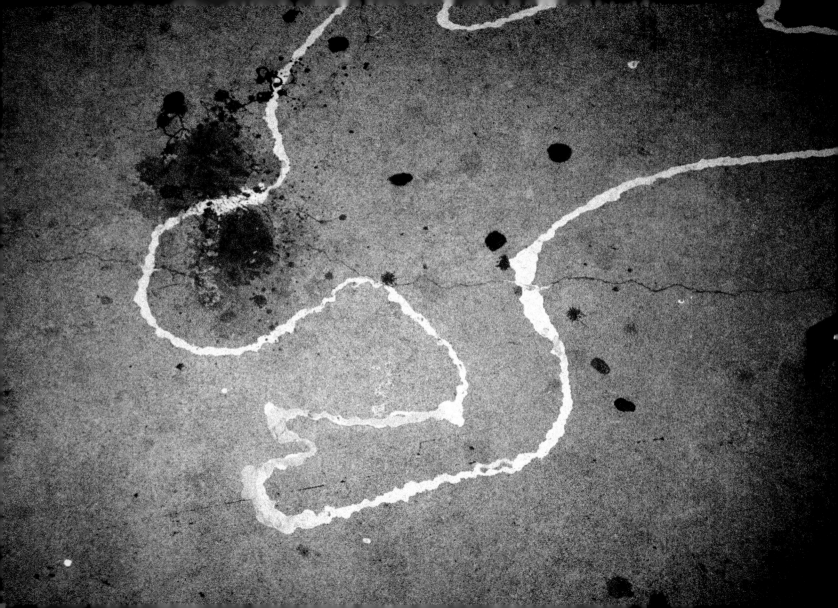

It's A ReLaxed BRutaLity.

he's let the FiNer things
in Life get the Best of him.

JAMES

SKETCHES ON THE ROAD

When trying to describe my life as a guitar player in a successful rock band I am always fearful of coming off like a jerk. Being on the road for pretty much three-and-a-half years straight, well, it's hard to process. First things first, it becomes ordinary to talk about and experience extraordinary things. Like when I am telling an old friend that we are opening for the Rolling Stones, which is very exciting for me; I can sound like I'm gloating. Or maybe I've already been talking about it for a while and there isn't much enthusiasm left in my voice. Then I sound jaded, like an ungrateful prick who's taking this all for granted. So it's difficult to explain in person and it's even harder to write about when you haven't done much writing since college, but here goes.

I want to describe as accurately as I can what it's like to be on the road. Like many things, I found that there were the beautiful pros and the inescapable cons. For every positive aspect, there exists its evil twin. It's the great balance of the universe manifest right here in this book, the yin and the yang, the hill and the valley, sunshine and rain. But before I get into it all, I think it's important to thank on behalf of the band all of the incredibly hard-working crew members who make these tours possible in the first place. Without them, and without you, there wouldn't even be anything for me to write about.

WINNING FRIENDS AND INFLUENCING PEOPLE

We meet a ton of people. The whole traveling-the-world, in-a-different-city-every-day-for-months-on-end thing brings us face to face with all types of people from all walks of life. On tour, you're the center of attention. Everybody wants to meet you. Great, right? I love meeting people.

I also enjoy the camaraderie with the other musicians from other acts on the tour. I set out early on in my life to learn as much as I could from as many musicians as I could. First, there is the technical knowledge you can glean. I spent a lot of time hanging around guitar techs, annoying them with questions about the guitars, pedals, and amps they used. Then there is everything you can learn by watching performances night after night. We have been able to see so many amazing shows I can't even begin to mention them individually for fear of leaving one out. It's amazing to see multiple performances by one artist as well, seeing how they vary or don't vary from night to night. You can also be inspired in a different way by watching bad performances, seeing how not to do things.

Being among new people every day creates some unique situations. For a while you can talk without any of the pretenses you have with your friends at home. You become an idealized version of yourself. You make changes to your identity without fear of repercussion. If your old friends were around you, they would bust you on a lot of the shit you've said; in fact, you wouldn't have been able to say it at all.

What's weird is, you can start to incrementally move further away from the person you really are, slipping away from the values you once guarded so closely. As more and more people come at you with the "star treatment," you can begin to feel entitled to it. Each day brings a new city, a new slew of people. For this reason I am glad to be in a band. Within our egalitarian system you can never become completely ridiculous. We keep each other in check.

Then there's the inevitable burnout. Faces start to blur. Your brain shuts down in protest over trying to process so many names and you strain to be polite as you see the disappointment in their eyes, but you simply can't take anymore. I understand, though, because I've been on the other side. I would wait outside of any show that came through Nebraska to meet the musicians. I hoped to gain some insight into these people because they'd produced things that I was so intimately familiar with. If you like the music, it makes you feel like you know the artist. I hoped to make some sort of connection so I would ask questions, but often only received a checked-out robotic response. Now I get it. They'd talked about these same things a million times. Sometimes, the imagined connection isn't even that deep. It's just that someone has seen you on television or in a magazine and you're a familiar face, part of this far-off magical world. But I understand this too. My first days in L.A. were filled with this fascination of being so close to things I saw in the media.

PLAYING MUSIC FOR A LIVING VS. LIVING IN ORDER TO BE ABLE TO PLAY MUSIC.
Performing onstage is the biggest perk of being a musician, my favorite thing to do over all others. Being able to do it on a nightly basis in front of an eager and adoring audience is one of the great blessings of my life. I got addicted to the buzz of performing early on at the house parties my first band, Montag, would play in suburban Lincoln, Nebraska, and it started me down a path of playing wherever and whenever I could. I would play at wedding receptions and country clubs, in jazz or rock bands. These "background music" gigs were an important part of my musical development. Because people weren't listening I had the freedom to try anything I wanted. I remember the shock I felt when my band, Square, developed an audience that actually paid attention to what we were playing, even singing along to the songs. Suddenly we were out front. Now, I watch thousands of people sing along every night. It's an amazing, almost indescribable feeling. As the lights go down and the energy in the audience starts to build, I feel that vibration in my chest, something like the rush you feel just before a first kiss with someone you genuinely like.

My life has always centered on music, but, from an early age, I was making other plans in order to make a living as everyone around me told me that music was an impractical career choice. Even my guitar mentor told me, "You should get a real job. This life is really hard." I decided to major in advertising when I enrolled at the University of Nebraska, figuring it was a creative yet practical career. Everyone was surprised I wasn't majoring in music. I figured that if a career happened in music, it would happen but I better have a backup plan. I was playing more music than ever, though, and soon realized that I could not pretend to be serious about advertising.

I can now play whenever I want. I have access to all of the equipment I used to drool over in catalogs when I was a kid. I have been able to meet many of my heroes, and have actual meaningful conversations with them. We get to go out on tour and play to substantial audiences every night. When I started, it didn't matter if anyone was there, let alone listening. I am completely grateful for this blessed opportunity. The truth is, sometimes it was easier when no one was listening. It didn't matter if we messed up—we would go further, take more chances.

WORLD PARTY

Seeing the world has been one of the most amazing aspects of this whole experience. It's strange, but I always held off on traveling overseas because I somehow knew that playing music would take me there. I had never traveled outside the country before we started touring. While I was growing up, my father traveled the world as the manager of international sales for a company in Nebraska. He took each of the Valentine children on trips with him. I was the second youngest of five. He was laid off before it was my turn. I have more than made up for it at this point.

Before touring, every city seemed distinct to me. Just traveling from Lincoln to Kansas City felt like moving between dimensions. That has changed. I now have to remind myself which continent I am on. Perhaps it's a subconscious adjustment I have made to keep from losing my mind. It is such a startling feeling to wake up and have no idea where you are. That happens a lot.

We have really been able to see how the world has been flattened by globalization. Every major city has the same KFC, Pizza Hut, and GAP stores. Local culture has been obliterated by mass media as well. The sixteen-year-old girls who come to our shows in Denmark are wearing the same clothes as the girls who came to see us in Austin, Texas, because they all watched the same Gwen Stefani video. The world seems really small in this way. It becomes more and more challenging to experience the uniqueness of these cultures.

While seeing the world has been tremendous, our success has unfortunately put more barriers in front of experiencing the cities we visit. In our early days we would usually meet most of the people who had come to see us (not hard when there were only a dozen or so people there). We may even have ended up sleeping on their couches. Often before or after shows I would hop in the car of a complete stranger and end up at some random house party or dive bar. These would be my own mini adventures to break up the monotony of backstage areas and hotels. Now often I feel trapped backstage, completely detached from these cities and people, because every backstage looks the same. In fact, every city ends up looking the same. A Groundhog's Day sort of thing starts happening. The strain of touring means you're often too exhausted to escape the protected bubble, so you often end up bored and frustrated.

Of course, the biggest downside of constant traveling is being away from family and friends. It's challenging to try to keep in touch with everyone, especially if you don't like talking on the phone, as I don't. While you want to keep everyone abreast, you get sick of describing the same things over and over again.

When you return home, you feel disconnected. There's a strange period of readjustment that was first described to me as post-tour depression. All of a sudden you don't have a tour manager waking you up and telling you where to be. Suddenly you have to decide what you are going to do. You also miss the buzz of being onstage every night and realize that your apartment is not a hotel room and you won't be packing up and leaving in the morning. Slowly you reconnect with your friends and find a routine—or maybe not. We were so busy over the last few years that we were never home long enough to get back into any sort of routine. We all went a little crazy.

Our friendship has really sustained us through all of this craziness. I know bands use this comparison often, but I feel like my bandmates are more brothers than friends. Our shared experience has forged a closeness I can only compare to family. And we're a functional one. When there are problems, we work them out right away. At first, it took me a while to get used to how much we would talk about everything, to the point where I'd get annoyed. But it's clear to me that this ability to openly communicate is what's held us together. I think you can see all of that in this book.

UK

It'll Be a goddamn Beautiful MUTINY.

Oh Shit, do we have to drive on the wrong side of the road?
It's okay, where we're going we don't need lanes.

Ok, so on that Note, ..
I Need to Ask For Your Name again,

137

He wants to Be seen, ☞ wait until
your career is over and you'll want
to Be seen too,

toast of the TOWN tonight, toast TOMORROW.

SUN MAROON 5 SOLD OUT

Most of the third ALBum won't Be PERfoRMABle.
things Like the Sounds of Demons CRYing...

certainty is the most dangerous thing in the world.

- Are you sure about that?

yes.

DeLiRiUM is a gReat thing FoR us, we weaR it well.

EUR
OPE

LOUDNESS

creating and analyzing are two different processes. Don't try to do them both at the same time or you'll hurt yourself.

if one of us was a tiger,
we'd all be in danger

KEEP CLOSED WHEN NOT IN USE

MAROON5

Thursday, October 14, 2004   London, Eng
                                           PST = 8 hours

Shepard's Bush

Lunch	1:00pm
Soundcheck	4:30pm
Dinner	5:30pm
Doors	7:00pm
Johnathan Rice	7:30 - 7:55
The Like	8:00 - 8:30
MAROON5	9:00pm
Curfew	11:00pm

that PART's wRong.
It's Beautifully wRong.

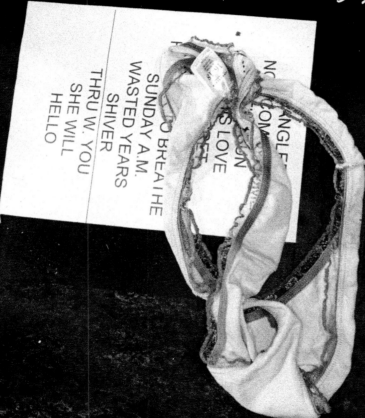

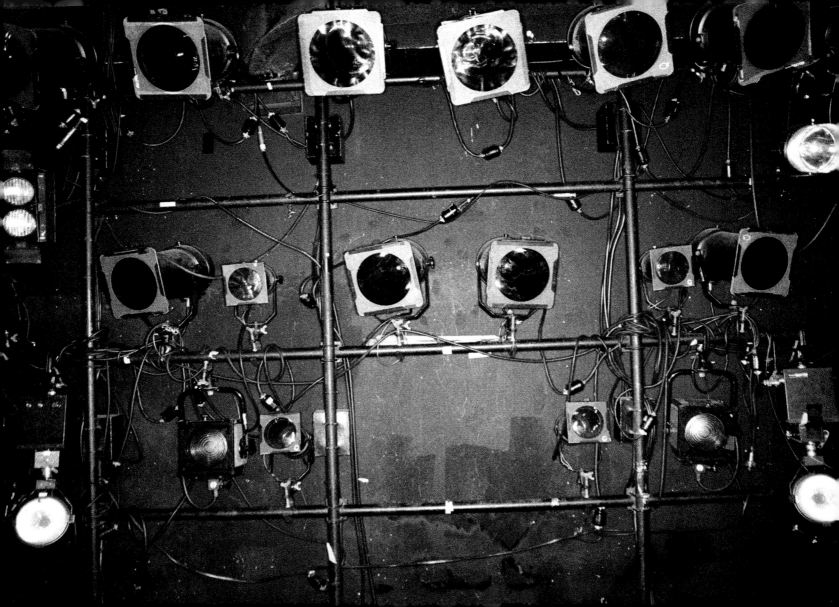

It's a Race to the Chorus and the Winner gets the solo.

MAGIC MUSHROOMS

MEXICAN
A happy trip. You laugh a lot and you feel awake and energetic.
Your senses become more clear, colours become more vibrant,
and things look funny ! You feel like you are walking on clouds! You
perceive everything different, time, distance, smells...
Recommended for first-time users. Social and controlable. € 11,95

THAI
Same effects as Mexican but the visual effects are stronger.
Colours are brighter and you experience more optic effects. € 11,95

COLOMBIAN
A lot of laughing like Thai but more visual effect, much stronger
and intense. Things you see can be blurred and distorted.   € 14,95

EQUADORIAN
Hallucinating like the Hawaiian but also lots of laughter and
energy. Great combination of having some fun while experiencing
hallucinations.   € 14,95

HAWAIIAN (COPOLANDIA)
This is a strong visual psychoactive trip for the experienced user.
Colours and details become intenser and transform into
hallucinations. A very clear visual trip.   € 17,95

MUSHROOM GROW-KIT
Grow mushrooms in only 2 weeks! Produces up to 900 grams of
mushrooms (40 portions). Works in every home. Very easy. Legal
to take overseas.

The Mushroom Stabilizer is a capsule that takes you out of the
trip, back into reality !   For only € 2,50

Mushroom
Growkit

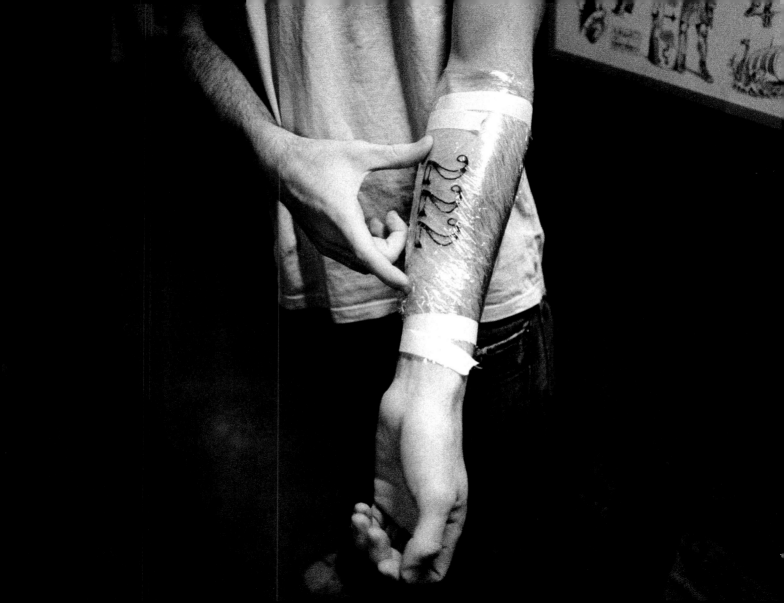

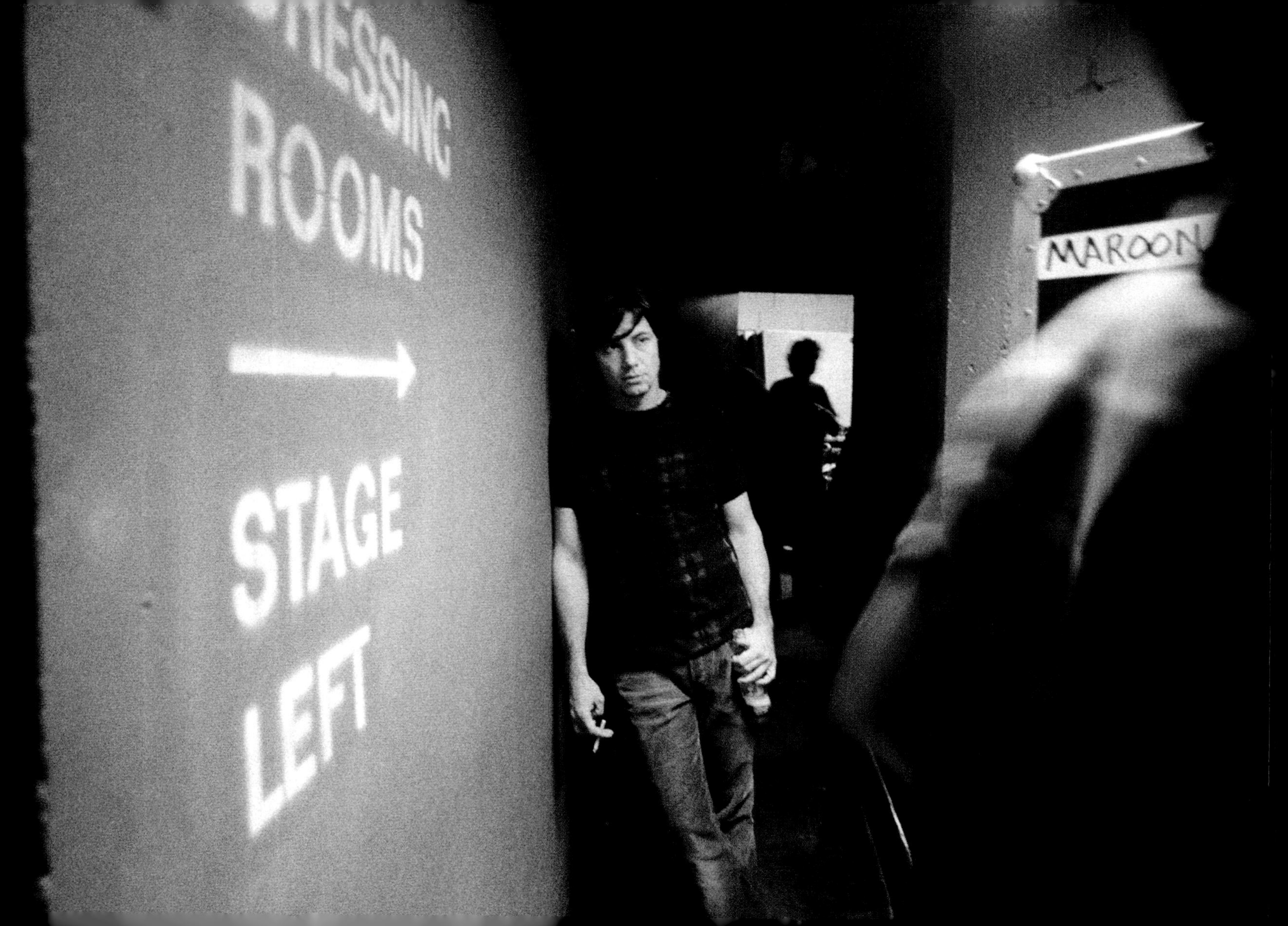
ROOMS
STAGE
LEFT
MAROON

time heals all wounds, even the one I'm about to give you.

→ JESSE

WOULD YOU RATHER BE DEAF OR BLIND? I don't even have to think about it for long and before I even get out of bed in the morning, before I roll out of my cavebunk, I have a blindfold tied around my head. I don't even know the name of the town we're in. It's just dark.

So how well do I know the bus? This is where we keep the bowls and this is the handle on the refrigerator. This sounds like a box of Grape-Nuts. *Here is my handle, here is my spout.* Things are different already. I'm alone in the front lounge, eating my breakfast and waiting for something to happen. I'm kind of helpless to leave the bus without a guide and am glad when the door opens and someone breathes his way inside. After the laugh, I know it's Mickey, and I'm glad about that. He understands. The night before in cold cold Minneapolis with James and some old friends from the area, the conversation turned to the question, "If you had to choose, would you rather be deaf or blind?" Today then, has turned out to be a day for experimentation. Mickey is just the man I'd like to lead me around at the start of my day without sight. I take hold of his shoulder and we make our way outside.

A college campus, that much I know, so I assume we're near the school's auditorium, maybe in an alleyway, maybe in front of the building. What does it really matter to me at this point? Mickey handles the introductions to the people who have arranged for this show, the kids in charge of student entertainment. What a fun night they've planned for us. I'm glad all of our lives have led us here to this moment . . . and the next, and the next. . . . These girls on the committee seem nice. I talk to them and shake their hands. I like the sound of her voice. Is she pretty? Her skin is smooth. The concept of beauty is interesting to consider in this new headspace.

Onward, to the bathroom, which I tell Mickey I can handle myself. In fact, I'll make my own way to the stage for soundcheck. On tour, sound-check is the definitive marker that means soon the sun will be gone and don't you wish you'd gotten up just a little earlier to enjoy the day. Sometimes, yes . . . but sometimes last night just had too many things to experience and learn from and enjoy that I didn't ever want it to end. I feel my way around the tile walls until I find the sink. It must be white porcelain with a silver faucet right? I can see it in my mind's eye as I feel the water on my hands. I can see those hands and how they are moving together. Now that I think about it, I can see it all in front of me. It's like radar—everything I hear helps me understand the room I'm in. Three hundered and sixty degrees around me I have a bubble of information.

Now I'm walking down the hallway toward the staircase I climbed earlier with Mickey. I've got my hand on the wall and my foot is waiting for there to be nothing beneath it. Ah yes, here we are, sliding down the wall toward the sounds of the drums on the stage. *Hello? Hi, I need some help getting up to the stage. I need to go behind the keyboards up there. Thank you . . . thanks for helping me. Yes, I know the blindfold is weird.* I'm ok with this type of weird. And now . . . here I am. It feels familiar. I know where all the keyboards are. I like the sound of this. Focus. Hear the note you want . . . no that's not it . . . that's too low . . . how low? . . . a minor third too low . . . I know this. I can hear this . . . I can feel this . . . this is a part of me. This soundcheck is different, more exciting. I know James is there when he shows up in my head as a chord joining what I'm playing. Adam's voice is comforting and I get wrapped up more physically than I usually do by what we're all playing together. I find my microphone slowly with my face and am able to communicate with everyone. What a joy. *Hello, guys. May I please have some more bass and kick drum in my wedges? Thank you. Beautiful. Perfect.* We're done and now the part of the day where we eat is upon us.

Let's take a walk in the cold wind and the light rain over to the dining hall. Outside, between Mickey and James, we're in open space, nothing in front of us. Do I want to run with them? We take off into the craziest feeling with the ground stomping in my ears and the wind and the rain and the rush. Now alone as they let go of my arms and tell me there's nothing in front of me but flat ground. I trust them and run by myself. It is freedom and joy and fear . . . but mostly fear.

Now, as I am sitting at our table with plates of food to feel and eat, I realize just how different today is. The conversations sound more intense, so they feel more intense, and become more intense. Everything seems focused, because everything is happening slowly. But everything is manageable. I'm still eating when everyone wants to take off for some free time before the show starts. "Free time" is a strange term. It makes me think, "Just how are we paying for the time that doesn't feel free?" *So long, guys. I'll make my own way back to the bus when I'm finished here.* A stranger lets me take her arm for the walk home and we talk about life on campus and life on the road. I don't remember her name. I don't remember a lot of details about a lot of things. I just hope that anything I'm supposed to remember is going to stick with me.

Here I am, surrounded by my bros as we walk to the backstage room for those moments of restlessness and anticipation before the actual moment begins. And now it's time to move toward the screaming. With the help of Teal, our guitar tech, I get behind the keyboards and soak it all in for a moment as I listen to everyone checking their sounds, those quick bursts of reassuring noise that let you know that as soon as it all starts you will be a part of it. Then, as Ryan clicks off the countdown for "Not Coming Home," I tear off the blindfold for the first time in ten hours. It's an explosion of light. My head is swimming in colors and shapes and movement. Suddenly, oddly, everything sounds different. I'm seeing things for the first time, and that's kind of contagious for my ears. The songs sound almost as if I'm hearing them for the first time.

I realize now that there's no way to stop the brain from filling things in when it doesn't know exactly what is in front of it. So when I was walking blind, as far as I was concerned that staircase handle was brass and the carpet was a dark red and this ceiling was vaulted and the design was modern and sleek and this stage was wood and the monitor board was to my left. But no and no, and no, and no, and on and on. They were all something else. Now there's got to be a period of reconciliation where the brain accepts its mistakes and acclimates to a new reality. While it's fighting it, there's gonna be some dissonance and disorientation and confusion. But once it sees what's really going on, there's just gonna be excitement and joy and love.

I'm gonna take it easy
for All you guys tonight.

Well I'm jaded, which I guess would mean I've formed an opinion on the subject.

He's everything you need in a tour Manager.
He can Be as gentle as the Rain
OR as Mighty as ThundeR.

Are you in the past
or are you in the Future?

- What, right now?

←

I wouldn't do that, I hit things FOR a Living.

R   Y   B

LET ME GO HOME NOW

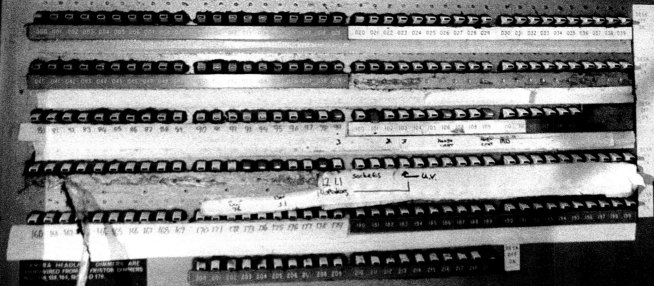

NORTH AMERICA

Everything →

→ ADAM

WHEN IT CAME TIME TO WRITE MY PIECE for this book, I realized I had no idea what to say, or rather, how to put down what has been happening to me over the past few years. I figure, why not just spout out my real emotions as they come? I'm sure my words will be properly edited and chopped so that I sound coherent and articulate. Anyway, I . . .

. . . just can't believe this moment is actually upon me.

contributed to writing two number-one hits.

have two new siblings *(a brother, Sam, and a sister, Liza)*.

fell in love.

fell out of love.

won a Grammy.

lost an aunt and an uncle. *(Marjorie Williams and Jack Cooper, two people who made indelible impressions on my life in almost completely opposite ways.)*

became a relatively well-adjusted adult.

am plagued with that overwhelming pressure of delivering it all again.

have never been more excited, turned on, and energized about life.

am extraordinarily lucky and grateful for the amazing life I've been given.

feel things more than ever.

lost a drummer, but, hopefully, not a friend.

have grown weary of politics and try to avoid them at all costs.

traveled and seen a pretty substantial chunk of the world.

watched the world around me expand.

continue to be a sponge.

continue to try to open my mind more everyday.

have an unbelievable group of friends, my extended family. *(They know who they are.)*

got a golden retriever named Frankie who is one of the best creatures in the world.

That's a pretty decent summation of what my life has been like over the past three years. The band and I are currently in the process of putting together our next record. I can't wait. I can't promise brilliant or transcendent or groundbreaking, but it's going to be fucking good. I promise some fresh sounds. We're going to be working with some amazing people. Something else I can't wait for is to continue my love affair with the fans at our shows. We performed at a casino in Connecticut on New Year's Eve and it had been so long since we'd played a show that when we walked out there I really didn't know what to expect. Then I felt the love from our fans, could literally feel it coursing through my veins. I was so happy to be playing again. Our next tour will be intense. I have a feeling that connection will go deeper.

I'm out of words and off to practice. Thank you for appreciating what we do. You've made our lives. For that, I am eternally grateful.

Basically, we're moving at speeds heretofore unimaginable.

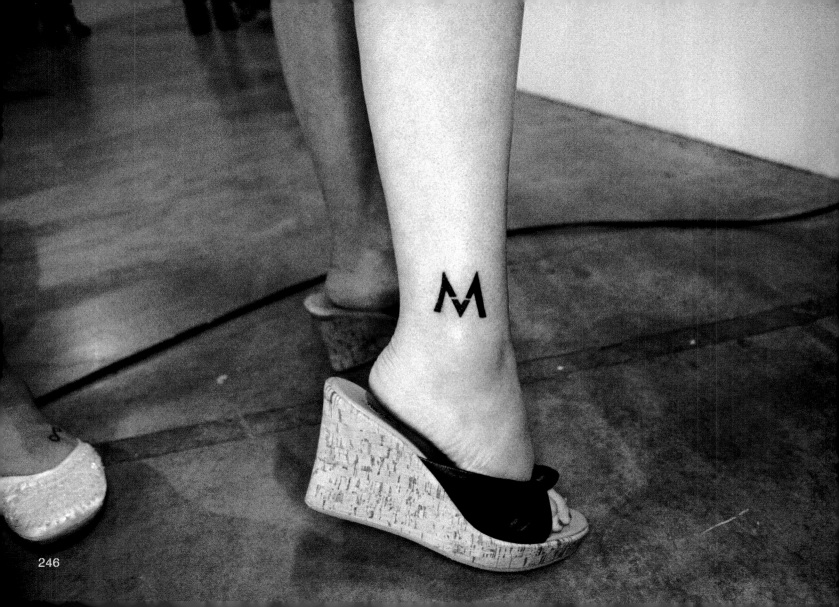

TOO MUCH METAL
for ONE HAND.

toomuchmetal.com

Yeah, I've got some new shady FRiends in New York.

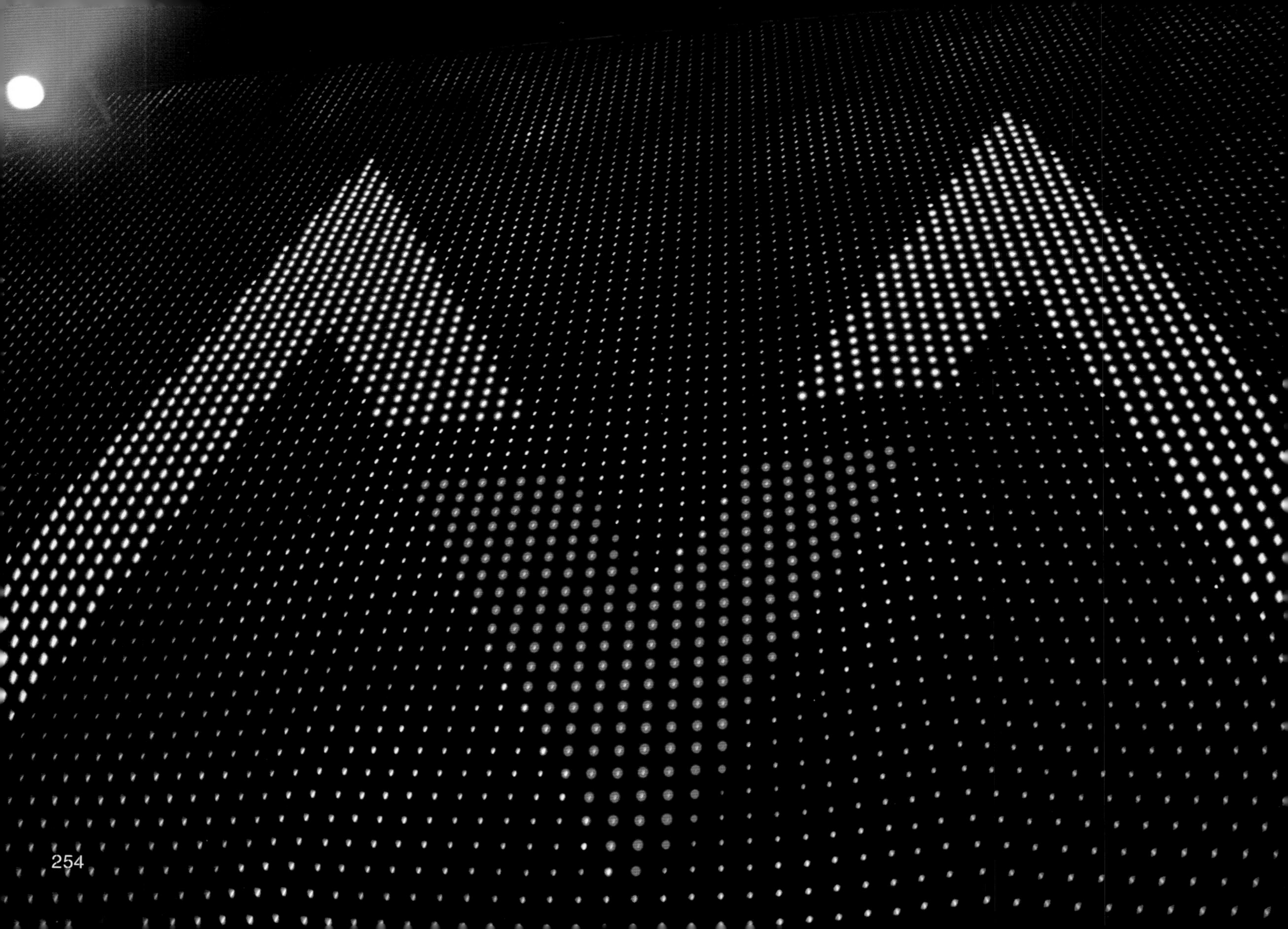

we're civilized men.

– Well, we're working on it.

Well,
we have it on tape.
Nothing to worry about.

It's Not cigarette smoke, it's Rock Fog.

Just think of how easy it is to overstay your welcome in pop culture.

Just hold the BUTTON DowN Man, hold the BuTToN hard.

I have several Films in Production,
And they're all coming out tomorrow.

You don't get to see the scenery,
you just get to meet the People.

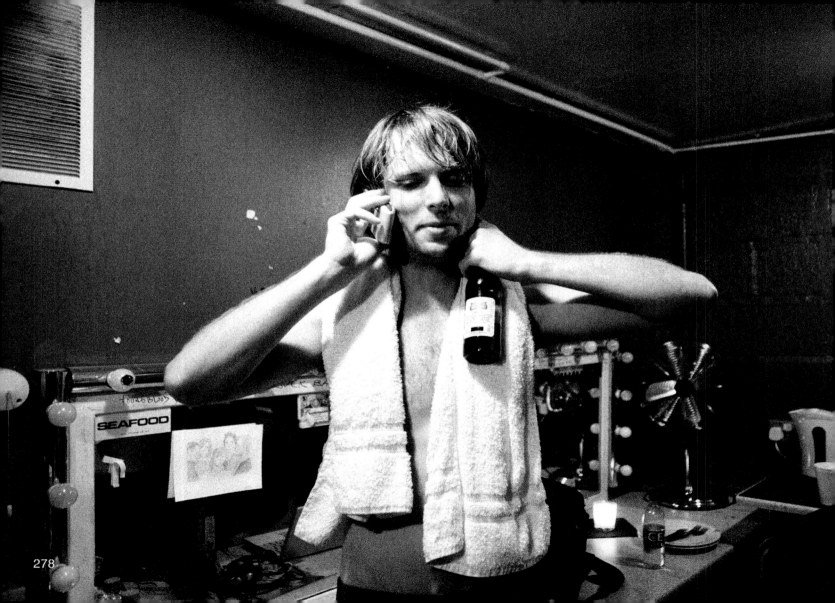

A

Pulp Fiction Intro

1. Shiver   GTR 3
2. Through With You
3. Tangled
4. Harder To Breathe
5. The Sun   Jimmy Solo + Ride
6. Wasted Years
7. Secret   SN II
8. Not Coming Home   GTR +
9. This Love
10.   Must Get Out
11.   Can't Stop   GTR +, MATT. Nord 96
12.   Sunday Morning
13.   Sweetest Goodbye   GTR +

14.   Cover
15.   She Will Be Loved   keys GTR

Thursday, April 14, 2005 AUBURN HILLS, MI

MY Life has already exceeded
MY expectations and I've had
to come up with new ones.